Dedicated To:

Lou Emma Jamison
Cathy Gaskins
Latesha Gaskins
Sheri Chanroo Gaskins
Joslyn Giles
Adrienne Blake
Andrea Woodfolk

What Daddy Never Told His Little Girl

TONY ALLEN GASKINS JR.

Bloomington, IN  Milton Keynes, UK

AuthorHouse™
1663 Liberty Drive, Suite 200
Bloomington, IN 47403
www.authorhouse.com
Phone: 1-800-839-8640

AuthorHouse™ UK Ltd.
500 Avebury Boulevard
Central Milton Keynes, MK9 2BE
www.authorhouse.co.uk
Phone: 08001974150

First published by AuthorHouse 1/30/2007

ISBN: 978-1-4259-9549-2 (sc)

*Printed in the United States of America
Bloomington, Indiana*

This book is printed on acid-free paper.

TABLE OF CONTENTS

CHAPTER ONE

Why is there a double standard between men and women in regards to sex?

Just like every answer to almost any question, it lies in history. A wise man once said, "There is nothing new under the sun". In this day and time, the unwritten laws are the same as they were in the days of old. My mother put it best, "when it comes to the number of partners a woman has had to the number of partners a man has had, you have the zero and the hero". That statement is as simple as this, if a woman has numerous partners in our society she is a zero, but if a man has many partners he is the hero.

I am a firm believer in combining ones history plus their biography to find the makeup of that person. In this case, it would be the history of mankind plus the biography of each gender to find the makeup of each individual sex. If we take a close look into history (his-story), we will find the answer to this question and why this double edged sword has stabbed our societies across the globe. It's a universal law that sex is a sacred act for a woman and almost like a job for a man. Even in certain religions, such as Islam, a man may have more than one wife, but to each wife he is the only husband.

That doesn't make it right nor do I condone that, but I will break it down.

Men were created in the image of God and women were created as help-mates to the man according to the Bible. In order to populate the word, it was up to the man to be fruitful and multiply. A woman could not conceive of a child no other way but by a man. Let's look a little deeper. We began with Adam and Eve and they begat Cain and Able. Then Able was killed by Cain. Already you have two men and one woman. It was up to them to create more of their own kind. That would in essence consist of brothers and sisters sleeping together and one man sleeping with many women to impregnate them, since the ratio of men to women wasn't equal and it would never be. If you notice in the genealogy of the Bible women weren't listed. It would read Adam begat Seth and Seth begat Enos and Enos begat Cainan and so on and so on. Already in the book of the law that our nation lives by, women were not even counted. They were mere vessels used to reproduce and sustain human life. The man was the ruler, the head or whatever royal title one may give him. At that time, replenishing the earth generation after generation was a job. It was a duty given to man by God. He said go forth and be fruitful. This was a direct order from God to man to spread himself out and replenish the earth with his own likeness. Fathers would have to sleep with daughters to keep the line going. As disgusting as it may seem to people of our time, this is what we are taught and what I accept as my truth. Picture this, a man not only sleeping with his wife, but his daughter and his granddaughters. A brother not only sleeping with his sisters but his nieces also, this is how our world began. From the beginning of time, you see the patterns of men sleeping with numerous women to reproduce as many of his likeness as he could. This was accepted and appreciated in that time.

I would like to remind you of the story in the Bible about Abraham and Sarah. God promised Abraham a child but Sarah could not bare children for many years. Therefore Sarah instructed Abraham to partake in this "sacred" act with the hand-maid. Abraham did so and they produced offspring of their own. It doesn't end there. Abraham still went back to Sarah and continued trying and finally God's promise was fulfilled and they begat Isaac. Once again, you see a man of God sleeping with numerous women for the cause of mankind. I repeat a man of God. This is what women expected and accepted.

Also in that time, Kings had a Queen and many other wives too. A King was known to have as many as a thousand wives. This meant that by our calendar year a King could sleep with a different woman every day for over two whole years. It gets deeper, not only could he have that many wives but he would have around 300 concubines. These women weren't even wives; these were like women on the side as we would refer to them today. You see the answer isn't in America or our world in this present day. We are living in the furthest most diluted version of what was harmless and accepted in the days of old. The answer lies within history. Are you beginning to see the double standard?

As time went on, different races and different regions would differ on this subject and make laws that may prohibit a man from having more than one wife. An average man wasn't granted that privilege or at least it wasn't recorded often. We look today and see that there are no Kings in our country and a President is our form of a King but there is no clause in our laws that allow him to have more than one wife. In fact, the only thing that may allow that is ones religion and in our nation those religions aren't what our nation is built on. Our nation is built on Christian foundations, where a man belongs to a woman and a woman belongs to a man. Once entered in holy matrimony not only is it a sin but it is against the law to sleep outside of that marriage. One would ask, why is it still seen as ok for a man to sleep with many women and in a sense it's a goal to see how many they can sleep with. The answer is simple; although laws have changed, the heart of man is still the same. Until God can change the heart of a man it will always remain the same. Now in this day and age, we see a more vulgar use of a man's body. But because of the laws we have in place it seems as if the double standard should no longer exist. Here's what happens, the essence of reproduction was lost just like the essence of sex itself was lost over time. We began with men and women and now we have gays and lesbians. Overtime, the essence of everything that God set in motion will be lost and replaced with a new more rebellious rampage without a cause. Similar to how we came about Sodom and Gomorrah, through evolution we will eventually leave out the blueprint that it began with and it will end up a modern day rendition of what it use to be. When we look at sex and the double standard, we realize there shouldn't still be one because there is no need for reproduction because the world has now been over populated, but the wheels have already been set in motion. This has created the snowball effect in the gap of sexual morals between men and women and we have reached the point of no return. But because of what our world was founded on and because of what was passed down we live in that same pattern. In this day and time, it is still seen so much worse for a woman to be promiscuous than if a man were to be.

Let's look at the symbolization of a woman's body in a deeper way. The woman was made from man so therefore in a way she belonged to the man, one man. Although a woman was one of a thousand wives, she was only for that man. Women were groomed and trained to be a man's wife all their life. Women married and bore children at early ages. Because there were so many more women than men, one man could be with many women sexually because it was normal and apart of life. They knew the structure of the world when it came to reproduction of man kind. It was no mystery or no secret that men slept with many different women. If it were ever the other way around, a woman did it because she was cast out and needed the money. Even in the days of the Bible there was such thing as a harlot, in this day and time we would call her a whore. It only took one man to impregnate a woman, and after she found that man he is the only man she was expected to bare children from. This idea followed women into this day and time.

Diving deeper into the history lesson, I will now focus on how we are what we were made of. Although we have laws that prevent us from having more than one wife or cheating on our wife and moral standards set in place that convict promiscuity, who is to deny that we as men aren't inevitably tied directly to a King who was able to have so many women? Who can deny that we do not have the same mind and the same body as those Kings? Who can say that we are not from the very lineage of men that were ordered to sow their seeds in numerous women? And what woman can say that she is not from the line of a Queen or a Princess? What woman can say she is not made up of the genes that made up women who were one of one thousand wives?

Granted, these times are not those of the old. Regardless, the same rules we were created to live by still govern our hearts today whether we like it or not. We as people are what we are and we as men are completely different from women when it comes to the ways of the heart, which decides the morals that we as a whole decide to live by. The reason is a man was not created the same as a woman and our gender roles are different. We are not made the same, our feelings and our emotions are constructed completely opposite. Men were made to hunt and to fight and to kill, therefore our hearts are not easily tied to one thing because at any given time you could have to forfeit that one thing you love the most. A woman on the other hand, was made to serve her man and be almost like a footstool in the days of old. A woman did not go out to battle she stayed back and kept the house and the children in order. A woman did not make decisions or call any shots. Because of this difference in our social roles our morals about sex are completely the opposite. A woman was a prize for a man after he had won a battle in a war or a duel against another man. A man was never a gift to a woman and that man could not be replaced with another man, but in an instant that woman could be replaced.

Therefore it is of the utmost importance for a woman to understand the makeup of a man and the history (his-story) plus the biography of mankind, to understand why there is a double standard when it comes to sex. Although women are empowered in this day and age, the fact that society was never conditioned for us to be seen as equals will always leave the scaled tipped to one side when it comes to sexual morality. Ask yourself this as a woman; "Do I want to be able to sleep with as many men as I can before I die to feel like more of a woman?" I can almost guarantee that majority of you say no. In fact the fewer men you sleep with the more you feel like a woman. But let a man ask himself "Do I want to be able to sleep with as many women as I can before I die?" And I can guarantee the majority of them will say yes to that question. That simple question shows that we do not think as equals so therefore what we hold sacred in our hearts and minds is completely different in many cases.

To sum it all up, a woman was made from the rib of a man therefore she is called woMAN. One woman belongs to one man but one man could belong to many women. Never could a woman have two husbands in any land and not even in religions is that condoned. Although it is not condoned for a man to have more than one woman in many different regions of the world, religions inside of those regions still believe that it is ok and who is to blame them for continuing in the way that the world was began. This is what was set in motion since the beginning of time and henceforth you have the double standard between men and women in regards to sex. So I ask you; do you want to sleep with as many men as you can? Or do you want men to sleep with as few women as we can?

CHAPTER TWO

Why is it that men don't appreciate celibacy, nor do they appreciate you after you've given in to sex?

If a man really likes you and cares about who you are and what you want then he'll respect your wishes, but if he only cares about himself and his personal needs then and only then can he not accept celibacy. Every woman should ask the man they are interested in about their feelings towards celibacy. This way you will see exactly what his intentions are or at least some signs of them. A genuine man or a relationship oriented man will wait for you. He may apply a little pressure but he'll wait. If a man says that he can't wait because he's a grown man and his body is accustomed to sex then he's in it for himself. Or if he says that since he's been having sex if he stops it will cause medical problems such as "blue balls", he's in it for himself. There are no harmful side effects that come along with celibacy. Watch out for the deep explanation that sex will bring you two closer and allow him to express feeling for you that words can't attain. That's a man who is use to dealing with this and women usually fall for it. I know a lot of men including myself that have been successful with that line after it has been applied just right.

One problem with practicing celibacy with a man you've just met is he may see you as a goal. It would be very hard to discern between a man that is genuine and a man that is goal driven. One difference would be the time factor. If he's genuine, he'll spend all the time he can getting to know you and asking questions about you while building trust. A goal oriented man's topic of conversation will be about sex or your reasons for celibacy. His phone calls will come far and few in between and when you do speak it won't be for long. Even though a man is goal driven, that doesn't mean he can't wait and in fact he may wait a long time for you. He could wait months but his time will be split up. He won't give you all of his time. He may get in touch with you when it is convenient for him and this may very well trick you into thinking he really likes you when really he's just waiting you out. On the other hand, a genuine man will talk with you or spend everyday with you getting to know you and getting nothing in return in regards to sex.

Be careful when you feel you're his goal! Play your cards right. Don't go in pretending to be one thing and then turn out to be another. Make a man earn his keep by staying strong in your beliefs and even if he's out to get you, you will end up getting him if you hold out and don't give in to sex. When you finally have sex with him he should have had to put in so much time that he doesn't ever want to leave you because he's so deep in love. One thing a man often forgets is that when you play with fire you can get burnt. He probably feels like he can engage in deep conversations on the regular and go on dates and still keep his heart distant from love, so while he's waiting for you to give him your innocence he's not catching feelings for you. But if you play your hand right that handsome young man that is goal seeking will fall in love and could give you the best love of your life.

I say that to say if you decide on celibacy make sure you don't change your mind before you can tell without a shadow of a doubt that he will do anything for you. Never use celibacy to get brownie points as a classy lady. If it's not what you really want don't fake it. Then you would be playing yourself! As soon as you say your celibate, the man goes into game mode. He'll bide his time and stay distant if he's not sincere. He won't call everyday and he won't talk long when he does. This is only because he doesn't want to give much of himself if he's getting nothing in return. When a man plays this role, it's because he is focusing on the women in his life that put out and only calling you when they can't be reached. The crazy thing is, usually when a man plays this roll the woman falls for him. This is because its human nature to want what you can't have, or to want someone that doesn't want you back. You know as a woman when a man you've just met calls you three or four times a day, the man seems pushy. Just like the laws of physics, if he pushes towards you then you move in the opposite direction. But when he plays it cool and pulls away, it draws you closer to him. Strange but true, that is why women are known for falling for the bad guys or the thugs. A man with a demanding schedule, like the life that comes with the streets, doesn't have much time for you. A certain part of you likes that because you have the freedom you need and you don't have to be bothered all the time. At the same time you begin to long for that man. You question yourself, "Why isn't he feeling me, is it because I'm not giving it up?" This absence makes the heart grow fonder if it is accompanied by a sexual attraction. To question yourself is the worst thing you can do. If he doesn't call, then you know right away he's not serious. Never think he's too busy, no matter what a man has to do, if he likes you he can make time for you. Don't sweat the small stuff. If he doesn't come to you, then don't chase him. If he only calls you every other day, don't give in thinking that it's because you aren't good enough or that he doesn't like you. Stay steadfast in your decision on celibacy and force him to play by your rules. Soon you'll see his true colors.

I call it the three month rule. The average player or "go getter" won't wait longer than that. I've never seen it done. A player may wait a month and if you haven't gave it up yet, then most likely you'll witness him move on. But if you show signs of weakness as if you're getting closer to giving in then that will keep him around but at a distance. So stay just as strong as you were on the day you decided to be celibate.

Now if a man has been talking to you EVERYDAY and you reach the three month mark, I would bet my bottom dollar he is for real. Meaning he isn't obligated to another woman whole heartedly and if he has one he is willing to leave her for you. He also respects your decisions and you as a person. That doesn't mean he's not having sex. A man will easily respect your wishes to be celibate, but that does not mean he will accept the same standards for himself. Therefore, he may be fulfilling his lust elsewhere. You can never be 100% sure about anything, but time will tell like they say. To test men, use no other weapon but TIME. Blessed are those who wait and cursed are those who rush. That goes to say that a man who can wait has a good heart although he is not perfect, he can be molded. A man who is in it for himself or just out to cheat on his girlfriend or wife won't waste much time on you. I say all that to say, DON'T PLAY YOURSELF!

You as a woman should respect yourself as a priceless piece of art. Honor yourself as a virtuous woman and never give in to insecurities and let your guards down. Don't ever feel like you owe a man anything. A man knows he has to work to get what he wants in any area of his life, so we expect to have to work to get a woman. Many women give in to a man because he buys flowers or spends money at the mall. That is the reason he does it, because he knows it will give you a guilty feeling like you owe him something. Since you don't have the money, you may repay him with sex or some type of intimacy. This is not necessary and a man does not respect a woman who pays him back in that way. Respect yourself and let him go to the moon and back and don't give anything sexual as repayment. If you are not asking for his time or his gifts then you do not owe him anything in return.

Many men will see you as a challenge and as a man that's what we live for. It is a man's nature to fight, challenge, bet, and take chances. Look into history all over the world. Across the globe men would have duels, battles, and all types of mono y mono competitions to prove who the better man is. Although this proved nothing at all, in society it was seen as a test of masculinity. Such is the same when it comes to women. If you say jokingly "I'm practicing celibacy", that man see's a challenge. He then will set in his mind that he is going to accept this challenge and not give it up until he is successful. Then the game begins. You go on dates to the movies and out to eat. You sit on the phone for hours and visit one another on occasion. You know in you heart you'll give in to sex if he pushes the right buttons while whispering the perfect lines.

Let's say it's been two and a half months. Your reaching your three month goal, but you're blinded so you can't tell if he's sincere or goal driven. You try to play it safe but you'll crash by default if what came out of your mouth doesn't line up with what is in your heart. Since he's goal driven he's being patient. He gets you in the right place that one night. Let's say, you've finally let him come over after midnight. Remember you've been claiming celibacy but you didn't mean it, you just wanted to seem classy. He sits and watches TV a little and talks to you softly and passes a few jokes. Then he asks about your day. You indulge in his false sincerity and open up very comfortably. He moves a little closer and puts his hand on your thigh. You see where it's going but you think nothing of it. The he leans in and kisses your neck. "Ooo that feels good", you say to yourself. He does it again as he rubs his hands up and down your thigh. He eases in between your thighs with his hand and heads straight to the spot. He gives a gentle swirl that sends chills through your legs. At the same time, he's still kissing your neck. Then he flips over in front of you and grabs the back of your shorts and gives them a tug. He's still greasing you up because his mechanical senses assure him that if he greases you up enough whatever he wants will slide right off. Before you know it, your shorts are coming off your ankles. But you're so gone because it's late, it's dark, and it feels so good. He has got you where he wants you. Knowing you already showered it's safe to say "can I lick it?" It's not because he wants to but because he knows that in order for him to get something, he first has to give something. You nod but without even acknowledging you, he's already on his way down. At this point, he knows it's going down. He pleases you the best he knows how and he knows this is the point of no return. All your inhibitions are out the window although a conviction can snap them back into perspective in an instant. But no matter what, you've gone too far. He's got a taste of your essence, your prized possession. Just like any woman, you think why climb if you can't climax? The tongue is good but your body knows God didn't make it for that. Your body calls for the instrument designed to fit you perfectly. He already knows that. He rises to enter into his land of milk and honey. He does just that! It may last long enough to send you up a wall or it may be so short it leaves you wanting more. But guess what, it doesn't matter anymore because YOU JUST PLAYED YOURSELF! You'll notice or if you've experienced this you noticed the haste in his departure and the decrease in his calls and the change of the content of your conversations, if this man was goal driven. Once you achieve one goal then logically you set new ones and try to achieve them. A goal oriented man will either leave you alone after that or set new goals for you. That goal may have been just to get it but the next may be to get it unprotected or on demand. Then the positions and the locations can be individual goals also. Please know a man's mind won't venture to far in this goal setting process. A catchy phrase in the white community relating to this is, "wam bam thank you maam". Appropriate huh? Remember when traveling an avenue of respect make sure what comes out of your mouth lines up with your heart. Be sincere about what you say you are or what you strive to be. Don't hold out for the fun of it because if you really want him you're going to give in and then the battle is lost. A one night stand can be on the first night or it can be after the first night you give up your innocence. If that's what the man wants then that is what he will get. So don't play with fire if you don't want to get burnt.

Celibacy is a choice and a noble one at that. Don't use the word in vein or your time will be in vein. Don't go to the point of no return because at that point your either going to give it or he is going to take it.

CHAPTER THREE

Can Guys and Girls be "Just Friends"?

Of course many people will read this and say yes, but I would say no and I have done surveys to prove my hypothesis to be correct. I do not believe in male and female "friendships", they always turn out to have some type of benefits. Henceforth we have the coined phrased "friends with benefits". This is very much common in our society because people start out as friends and end up being more than that. I do believe that the greatest foundation for any relationship is friendship. "Love without friendship as its foundation is like a mansion built on the sand". Therefore I would not stray away from cross gender friendships and in fact I would search for them if you are looking for a good relationship. The reasons men can not be a genuine friend to a female is because of our predator mentality, and the only exception to that rule is if the woman isn't attractive in any way. Literally the woman would have to be in a vegetable state for her male friend not to be attracted to her at any time.

I asked ten different women if they have had male friends. All ten said yes at one point in their life. Then I asked them if he ever made a sexual pass at her and all ten said yes at one time or another. Some women said it took years before he did, but it never failed. In life we live by margins. Majority rules, therefore with statistics we go by what majority says. Yes, there may be a few men that can be strictly friends but even if that were the case that man most likely doesn't like women. Those are the only true male friends and I'm sure that many women have had that homosexual male friend at one point. I've met those types of guys before and they are just like a female when it comes down to the way they carry themselves and the way they think. Since they are attracted to males they can be strictly friends with a female. In essence, it's just like that female having another female as her friend because he thinks and acts just as she does for the most part.

A lot of men play the friend role to get a woman. It's the best role to play in my opinion. It works better than the taken role, better than the gangster role, and better than the baller role. Beware of a man when he say's he just wants to be a friend. Here's how it goes. A man will introduce himself to you in a pleasant manner or is introduced to you in a harmless and calm setting. This man will engage in conversation with you all about you knowing that as a woman you need someone to just listen sometimes. He will go out to eat with you and chill with you in intimate settings but never try to be intimate. He'll say nice things and be the sweetest gentleman but all the while he never makes a sexual comment or tries to flirt. He'll seem just like a brother figure. Before you know it you'll find yourself confiding in him and trusting him with your every secret and thought. This is when he knows he has you on the ropes. If you get caught up in this you'll either get played for a fool or you'll meet the man of your dreams. I don't believe any man wants to be just friends. He see's you as prey but he knows in order to get you he may have to stalk you in the proper way. He will lay low and play his hand right waiting for the right time to make his move. You will find yourself opening up and letting your guard down. You'll share friendly hugs and walks in the park and things of that nature. All the while, you are growing fonder of this gentleman. Then you begin to form a trust in your friendship and this is where you are almost gone. The man will take his time. For different men it's different periods of time before he makes his move. For example, a quiet and reserved school boy could wait a year or more, but an outgoing and go getter type of man may wait two months. His ultimate goal is to make you feel so comfortable that you throw yourself onto him. If he is handsome or smooth enough he knows that he is capable of doing this. Now, if he isn't use to getting girls on demand then he knows he will have to wait until you are so comfortable with him that when he makes a move you like him so much you entrust your body in his hands. That's when it's the hardest for you as a woman because he has been so nice to you all of this time that even when he makes a pass you don't deem it as threatening so you let it slide. What you'll notice is that each pass will get a little more aggressive and if you don't stop him it'll end up in you two being very intimate. This is where friends with benefits begin. A lot of women just want a male friend to get the male perspective on life to help her with her man. And a lot of men will play that role just waiting for the day that you are down and out because your man has finally slipped up and broke your heart. Then he'll move in as the sweet and innocent prince charming and since you're in a vulnerable state of mind you may give in. I'm sure you can stop and remember the time this happened to you or almost happened to you. Just like the ten women I interviewed I'm sure that you have been through this same experience. You could look at it as a shame or it may just be something you can laugh off.

If you are at all attractive then no man can be just be your friend. He can try to and he may last a long time but he will eventually make his move. No matter how long it takes and don't get caught up in the amount of time he's gone without trying you. Just know that to a man a woman is prey and just like every predator you take your time when the prey that you really want and is very hard to catch. It's usually the beautiful or very classy women men try to befriend in order for them to let there guards down. If a woman has ever been told she is pretty in any way, shape, or form then that woman should automatically know that she can not befriend a man.   There are perks to having male friends though, so I wouldn't just push him away even though you know he doesn't want to be a genuine friend. Many relationships are physical and after the sex is boring and looks begin to fade then there is nothing left to stand on. But when you have friendship as your foundation you always have something to fall back on. If a man tries to be your friend allow him to do so but put him through the test. Don't let his little passes slip by and don't allow yourself to fall for him to soon. Be strong and stay focused because a handsome friend could very easily turn into prince charming. You know very well that there is no better feeling than having someone that is attractive that you can call on whenever you have a problem and be able to sit and talk and laugh for hours. To feel like your safe and that he is on your side and that you'll never have to worry about arguing, being beaten, or being cheated on. That's the greatest feeling in the world, even for a man. Everybody wants that type of friend. This is why this type of friendship could be rewarding. If a man has to pay his dues and he has to befriend you before he can become intimate with you then he appreciates you as a woman. If it's any other way a man can see you just like a piece of meat or prey as I call it. When a man has to put in genuine time and he is willing to do so that means that he is serious about what he is doing. Therefore, when he finally gets you if he ever gets you, he will appreciate you more than ever. You are his work of art, what you have is not something he bought or found on the street corner, but what you have is something he built and a man appreciates that more. That is why if you put a man to the test and he is forced to be genuine and forced to really get to know you as a person before anything physical happens he will love you for that. This is how long and healthy relationships are formed and this is why I believe in building a friendship before a physical relationship. A man who has to build something from the ground up will appreciate it much more than if it was just given to him. So when you meet a man and he wishes to befriend you make him build a relationship with you from the ground up. Don't give him anything but instead make him earn it. Therefore if you ever decide to give in to this man, regardless of his first intentions he will be hooked because of the work he has had to put in to get to that point. This is how you as a woman can find the love of your life. So many women make the mistake of just letting a man in her life by allowing him to claim her right off. When if she would have made him pay his dues she would have experienced what real love is all about. All love after friendship is not guaranteed nor is it forever, but it is better to have loved and lost then to have never loved at all. My mother always told me "the best of friends make the best of lovers". This meant so much to me after I found it to be true. When you have someone that you can just sit and laugh and talk with and never have to worry about kissing and touching or going to that point of no return, that is when you've found something special. So that way when you are old and tired and you have no desire to make love to that person you will still enjoy their company because you are able to be just friends.

If you have a male friend and you have asked yourself this same question then I would tell you to ask him. Communication is the key. Ask your male friend does he like you. Remember he's being your friend to wait you out, to draw you to him. He is in a sense the predator and you're the prey but he being your friend is to reverse the role and make you want him. So ask him, "Friend do you like me"? See what he says and go from there. Majority of the time he will be honest with you because this is what he wants. He wants you to wonder these things and he wants you to want these things. So therefore if you ask him then you are allowing him the opportunity to be real with you. Make sure that when you ask him you have a real friendship, for example don't ask after the first week or two wait a month or so. That is a sufficient amount of time to build a friendship that can go places.

When you allow him to open up then you are allowing your friendship to grow and grow in the right direction. When you know what you are dealing with then you know what to expect and this is one thing that you can expect a man to be honest about because this is what he wants all along. If he says he doesn't like you then he's lying and you know that you asked to early, so back off and give it a little while longer. When he says no, it doesn't mean he doesn't like you just mean he's not ready to admit it. So therefore in this case, time is of the essence. When you give a man time to build up feelings, it's only a matter of time before he explodes. So if you ask him before he makes a fool of himself then you've saved yourself a good friend and some embarrassment. After he's admitted to liking you just continue in the same direction you were already moving in but knowing and understanding that you are building something that can last a lifetime. Trust me, when a relationship is built on friendship it steps into a whole different realm of love and it has to be evaluated completely different from a relationship built on lust. Therefore many of the answers in this book may not be exact for a relationship built on friendship. When you build on this you are building a mansion that can be passed down the line. This is not conventional love, this is unconditional love. So continue what you have with your male friend and don't blame him when he is weakened by the overwhelming power of friendship. A powerful friendship has made a many men and women like their own kind, so you can only imagine what it can do if it's with the opposite sex.

Cherish what you have and know that if you play it smooth and take your time allowing love to take its natural course then you will find out that this is the greatest love you can ever have. If you just want a friend and you do not wish for this man to ever be your lover then I would suggest you have an open mind when befriending the opposite sex or just stick to female friends. Sometimes looks and money isn't what is best for you. True love has no face and its value is priceless, meaning that no amount of money can buy true love. And when you least expect it the ugliest or poorest man in the world could make you feel like the most important being on earth just by being your friend. So be safe and be smart when it comes to befriending a man, don't be afraid to just let it flow. You may go up and down or in and around, may have kids and marriages but a good friend will always be there and you never know when that seed of love will blossom and you'll reap your harvest. Be safe and be blessed!

CHAPTER FOUR

Why is it so hard for a man to express his feelings?

What a lot of women don't know is that when a man falls in love he almost never falls out of love. A woman has a built in recovery system unlike the man. Therefore a man protects his heart in a different way. Women can cry without shame or remorse. A man doesn't feel the same freedom to cry through his problems, it isn't manly in our society. Therefore in order not to end up crying, a man can't allow himself to get hurt. A man will hide his feelings as long as he can. For a woman to know a man loves her, she should feel it and not hear it. A good slogan to live by is "believe none of what you hear and only half of what you see". I would apply this because everything a man tells you may not be from his heart. When trying to understand a man's feelings make sure that you tread lightly. This is a vault that I hesitate to open because you may not want to know what is really inside.

We all know about the poker face. When playing poker one is taught not to let his expressions show what type of hand he has or the next move he will make. The same goes with a man in a relationship. We as men try to hide our emotions so that our woman never knows how we truly feel. That way she always has to try to understand us and as long as she is trying then we do not have to worry about her leaving. If a man would let his woman see exactly what he is feeling and that was her goal, then she has nothing left to see in him. Therefore, a man will stretch out this process as long as possible until he knows for a fact she is caught up. I was always told by my father that a woman is patient enough to play a role all the way up until marriage and then as soon as she gets that ring of security everything about her changes. When you think about it in other walks of life this is very true. Imagine fighting for a position at work or on a team. While you're fighting for that spot you give your all and nothing less. You always try to out do those around you so that you look better than they do. Then you finally win the spot you wanted so badly and there is no competition because you are what you wanted to be. Now you start to slack. You don't try as hard as you use to and you don't give the energy and dedication you use to. A man has this theory down to a science. As a man our defense mechanism is to hide our feelings so that we never let the woman know she can relax because we aren't going anywhere.

On the other hand, a man could not be telling you how he feels because he feels absolutely nothing. While a woman is being sincere and taking it all in, the man is brushing it off as just another day. As men we try not to sit and fantasize about marriage with kids and the deepest love. We inherently know that if we fall in love that it will take more than a disaster to make us fall out of love. Therefore, knowing that's the case we try our best to fight love for as long as we can. As a woman you could feel the world for the man your with and wonder everyday why he doesn't express his feelings or write you a letter to tell you how he feels. The reason is because he likes you so he doesn't want to lie to you. He knows it's a good possibility if he does he could end up hurting you because he's not ready for love. Therefore, he says nothing at all. When you wonder why your man isn't telling you how he feels, don't always brush it off as if he doesn't know how to, understand that he may not be feeling anything. As a man I would say it takes twice as long for us to fall in love. I've been in relationships that I didn't begin to truly love until after a year, but she had loved me since the second month. There is a difference in the feelings of men and women for a reason and the reason will be touched on in other chapters as well as this one.

Let me paint you a picture. You or a female you know may have this type of man. Your man could be starting to like you, but he's holding back. He takes feeling from past relationships and recycles them on you. This man may write poems and letters with deep meanings but in essence you don't feel that his feelings are really there yet. The thing is that he knows he has to express something because you're giving so much of yourself. If he doesn't give you something back then you'll feel like he doesn't like you. He knows you are wife material but he really doesn't want to let you know that. There is something about his expressions that let you know he's not being real. You may have a sense that he is just spittin game with his words or letters, but you can't just accuse him of that so you accept it one word at a time. The reason some men have to fake it is because he's not really feeling much yetl. He knows your pretty and that you have a nice body and all the features he likes, but that's all physical. For a long time your man will have a hard time pin pointing exactly what it is about you that he likes outside of your looks. All along you are beginning to fall head over heels for him because you're judging his qualities and not his looks.

You will find yourself shutting other men out and walking with your head in the clouds. Your man can see it in your eyes and feel it in your touch that you are all about him. There is probably nothing he could ask you for that you wouldn't do your best to get it. Be careful. When a man begins to feel like this he may put you to the test. This may scare him a little so he backs up and begins to treat you like a fling. He may not call everyday or wait for you to call him. After a little while you will begin to ask yourself if he really even likes you. Just know that if this happens to you, this is when a man is guarding his heart. He knows that if you are feeling like this then its time he begins to show you a little more feelings in order not to lose you. If he's smart he'll muster up some feelings and express them to you. Most likely since this is what you've been waiting on you'll buy right into them and that's not dumb of you. But at the same time he will continue to ignore the love that is forming so that it doesn't get the best of him. He knows your falling in love but he won't let himself fall so that way he will feel as if he has the upper hand. This man won't calculate the things you do for him because that would make him love you back. He'll sit back and act as if nothing is going on and let you fall deeper in love. While you're changing everything to perfection for him, he's sitting and watching every minute of it because he's not there yet. Some girls go as far as getting his name tattooed on them and deleting all the other guys' numbers out of their phones even if they were just friends. So if that's you please believe you're not alone.

You may have done all of the above and yet still didn't know how he truly felt, although you think you did. Think back and ask yourself if he was just all words and no actions, and were you all actions. If that's the case then he knows for sure that you love him with your all and if he leaves you'd be heart broken because of the things that you have sacrificed. At the same time because he hasn't really showed many actions of love if you left him you may not know if he really misses you and that would haunt you everyday. This is the security that every man wants and this is why men hold back. He wants to know you love him and wants you think he loves you. Every man feels that the things you are sacrificing are only to get him to love you whole heartedly. Therefore as a man he feels that if he shows you that he does then you'll stop doing the things you did to get him there. Most likely he's right and even you know that. So you may be reading this and you've experienced this or have seen it happen. You could have been with your man for a year or more and you still may not know what your man truly feels. That is something a man never wants to really give up. That's his money in the bank. He will continue to tell you just what you need to hear to keep you satisfied as his woman, but never reveal his deepest feelings that would give you the security that you've given him. You see, this is a man's defense mechanism. Your man will hide his feeling because he's ashamed to let you know you got him whipped. He knows that when it's real you will know its real and that's when you won't have to try anymore. It's simple, when you reach a goal you no longer have to try to reach. Therefore you let it go and set another goal.

Therefore when a man truly likes or loves a woman he won't express his true feelings because he doesn't want to lose her. Where men mess up is when they go to long without expressing their feelings and they let the woman slip away, but that's another book itself. As a woman, beware of a man that fills your head with poems and love letters. A lot of times when he is writing it's because he knows that's what you want but he may not feel that way at all. When a man holds back and you don't know what he feels, but a part of you can feel it, that's when you should cherish it. At that moment is when a man could be being most sincere and genuine. Knowledge is power and power turns into pride and pride comes before a fall. This is an unwritten law but every man's heart is programmed with that information.

To every woman who reads this, know your man! Don't wait on words because a lot of words could have no substance. Believe in actions. Silently actions speak louder than words. Look for a man's actions and that is how you will know he loves you. The Bible says you'll know the tree by the fruit it bares. A grapefruit tree won't produce oranges and an orange tree won't produce grapefruit. That goes to say a good man won't make you feel bad and a bad man won't make you feel good. So in watching for a man's actions, look for the man that will hold your hand in public, the man who will rub your back until you fall asleep, and the man who will cook breakfast for you in the morning. The amount of money a man spends on you or the nice places a man takes you means nothing. Those things take nothing of that man, but a man who gives of himself, a man who sacrifices his own time and feelings for yours, then that's the man who has real feelings. Many women focus on the wrong things and let the little things pass them by. It takes more of a man to get up and cook breakfast for you in the morning than it does for him to take you to a four star restaurant. If a man doesn't love you then he won't give of HIMSELF. It's important that you be able to tell the difference between a man giving of HIMSELF and a man just giving.

CHAPTER FIVE

Can the Beauty of A Woman Stop A Man from Cheating?

Beauty alone can not stop a man from cheating! Cheating is a decision not a reaction. The beauty of a woman would have to be inside and out and it would have to be flawless in order for a man to stop cheating. In other words, a woman with any insecurity would already fall out of that category of "perfect beauty". Picture this, Halle Berry and Beyonce Knowles being cheated on. That in itself could be a perfect picture that would answer this question right away, but its gets so much deeper than just those two names and that's where I would like to take you.

There is such thing as an unattractive woman and to understand why beauty can't stop a man from cheating you must understand what beauty is made up of in the mind of a man. . Before you get confused, I want to explain that when I say unattractive I don't mean butt ugly, I mean less attractive. For example, Beyonce is what I will consider attractive and Cicely Tyson would be less attractive or unattractive. So please don't get too caught up in the word choice, I'm just speaking left or right and nothing in the middle. Beauty is in the eye of the beholder, I'll give you that one. Most eyes of men behold pretty much the same thing. An unattractive woman may have more of a chance of having a faithful man than an attractive woman. The reason is because an unattractive woman lacks natural beauty, so she must compensate for that in other ways like a beautiful personality, a meek spirit, a passionate heart and a submissive will. Those qualities are not taught, they are picked up along the way. A woman either has them or she doesn't. Do you? The qualities that most unattractive women share are the qualities that speak to the heart of a man and not the penis of a man. Those qualities are what tie a man down and bind him by the neck. This unattractive woman grabs a man in a much deeper way than a woman with a beautiful face. This woman goes well beneath the surface of his rough exterior and grabs what is most dear to him. You see an unattractive woman will unknowingly make a man feel like a King just because of the qualities she has picked up along the way. This sense of control and manliness means so much more to a man than a pretty face. The feeling an unattractive woman may give a man can never be replaced because it takes him home. When I say home, I mean back to the beginning of time when a man was King and she was Queen. To the times when she was the heart and he was the head. This is where a man feels at home because this is how God created a man to exist. A man may meet an unattractive woman and become friends just to get a better idea on the female perspective of life and before you know it he could fall in love. It is true that when finding love with the heart, opposites attract. It's hard to fall in love with an unattractive woman because her lack of beauty may put up an extra barrier that he has to break through; but it's even harder to leave her alone after you've fallen for her. Its something about her qualities that lets you rest at ease. But its sad to say, when a man leaves a unattractive woman nine out of ten times its for a more attractive woman.

The difference in an attractive woman can be found and understood very easily. Let me break it down. She is beautiful so she gets doors opened and held for her, so she doesn't have to hold them herself. She is beautiful so she gets extra gifts on birthdays and holidays. She is beautiful so she gets extra food in the drive thru at McDonalds or she gets to skip the line at the club while the less attractive women wait in the cold or mosquitoes. These little perks slowly strip away her humility. Now she expects to be given free food, she expects to be skipped ahead in line and for the door to be held. Then when she is in a relationship because she is beautiful every man she dates feels he has to impress her or put her on a pedestal, therefore as he pushes her up all she can do is look down on him. This gives her a certain attitude that doesn't allow her to be submissive like she was as a little girl. Now she wants her way and she expects nothing less. This beautiful girl is slowly becoming a monster on the inside and the only time she is genuine is when she is alone. Over the years, her kindness and humility is scraped away and replaced with arrogance and a selfish spirit. What this beautiful girl doesn't realize is that her man hates almost every part of her but he can't over power her beauty. What she doesn't realize is that he enjoys being away from her to get a break. The only time he is truly happy is when she is quiet and they are walking and all the other men are lusting after what he has. This beautiful woman has filled her head up to believe that she is beautiful all the way through and can't see that she has no plausible qualities as a woman.

All that goes into play when a man cheats on a woman. There's more, there is something I like to call the one flaw rule. The rule states that if there is one thing wrong with you then that gives your man the room he needs to cheat. I know it's hard to swallow. Your saying to yourself, "how unfair, no one is perfect". And you're very right but such is life. You see man will sleep with a woman for one thing that he likes about her. You may be beautiful but he hates the fact that you can't cook, so he cheats with a woman that can. You may be beautiful but you have dark brown eyes, so he cheats with a woman with light brown eyes. You may be beautiful but you don't have the smallest waste with a big butt, so he cheats with a woman who does. Are you getting the picture? A man may sleep with this woman because she has green eyes, then he'll sleep with this woman because she has sexy thighs. Then he may sleep with this one because she can sing and this one because she has a degree, or this one because she drives a nice car. All it takes is one thing that he see's and likes and that will draw him in. That goes back to why a King would have so many wives, it only makes sense. Each woman is unique in her own way and no two are the same. Think about the possibilities a man has when choosing women; there is an endless supply. Just because you're beautiful doesn't mean a thing because there is always someone else who has something you don't and that's what keeps this vicious cycle going. Understand unless you're perfect in every single way shape or form, there is a possibility your man is going to cheat and if he is fly enough to get you then I can almost guarantee he'll want to get another one.

That ties right into the confidence theory. When a man can get a pretty woman it gives him all the confidence in the world. Just like in anything you do, if you do it once you feel like you can do it again. Don't feel like "oh he has me and I'm prettier than all these other girls so he won't want anyone else". That's the last thing that should cross your mind. Remember curiosity killed the cat. When a man gets one beautiful lady he automatically wonders if he can get another. Some pretty girls that have been cheated on say "I'm going to get a fat black guy who will never cheat on me because he appreciates my beauty". I witnessed a funny story when it comes to this. My sister once met a guy over the phone. She hadn't ever seen him but they were talking for months every single day. She grew to love him because he was so nice and so funny. He would treat her like a Queen; he would talk and laugh with her for hours on end. She felt like she was on top of the world because she finally found a man that respected her and treated her like she deserved to be treated. One day they finally met, he was about 6'5 and he weighed like 140 pounds. He was like a tall stick. He had on a very dingy outfit and he was very less fortunate. He had a huge birth mark in the middle of his face that killed any chance of him being attractive. Now, my sister was beautiful. She was about 5'4" and 115 pounds. She had hair that came to the middle of her back and she had a perfect smile and a beautiful face. Because she had already fallen in love she couldn't even tell how ugly he was. All she saw was a person who treated her like a Queen.

I will never forget him because he took her virginity and changed the way I saw guys like him. They dated for a while, I'd say about a year or longer. Throughout most of the relationship, he was prince charming but towards the one year mark things began to change. He was beginning to get use to this beautiful girl and he loved her as arm candy. He had taken her most prized possession and shelved it as his trophy. What happened was this chump had found his swagger. She gave him a profound confidence that radiated like the sun. All of a sudden, this ugly duck was the big swan of the pond. He began to attract other very beautiful women because they were wondering what it is he has that she wants. The other girls were drawn to this swagger. I promised it changed his life, he got a job so he could dress better and he even practiced harder so he could start on his varsity team that he had rode the bench prior to meeting my sister. Now you have this very unattractive guy, who had found himself through this beautiful girl and all of a sudden he was Morris Chestnut. He began to cheat on my sister with the other beautiful girls that had drawn to him. He started yelling and cursing her out just like the handsome jocks use to do and now he was just another guy. I shared that to show just how I formed my confidence theory and since then I've seen it over and over again. Take a second and remember when you saw it happen right before your own eyes.

Besides the one flaw rule and the confidence theory you have the almost impossibility to find a complete beautiful woman. For example, you have the rich beautiful woman and the poor beautiful woman. I use rich and poor in the same sense as attractive and unattractive. I'm not saying there isn't a middle, I'm just using the extremes so the examples don't go too far or dig to deep. The rich beautiful girl is catered to hand and foot and is brought up to expect that. She is arrogant and rude. She expects the finer things in life and will settle for nothing less. That's why they end up NFL or NBA wives. They will deal with the cheating and the beating as long as they can rock the Prada and Gucci. Rich beauty may date cute but most likely they will marry rich. If you are this woman this may sit right in your lap. So ask yourself these questions. Can I cook? Do I like to clean? Do I yell back at him when he yells at me? Do I curse at him? Do I ignore what he tells me to do and do what I want? Be honest with yourself, nobody is listening but you. Now, if you answered yes to all of those questions or all but one or two, that's why your beauty won't stop him from cheating!

Then you have the poor and beautiful. This is a touchy case because most of these women I've met have had so little resources or been through so much they still have trouble sleeping at night. Although most of the things they've experienced are not their fault, they suffer the consequences just as if they chose to be poor and beautiful. Most of the poor and beautiful women I've encountered had no father figure or positive role models in their life. They were from single parent homes where they couldn't be fully trained on how to be a classy lady. A lot of these women moved from place to place and their mother worked two and three jobs or worked nights. These beautiful ladies were left to the wolves we call men. These men began to rape and molest these young beautiful women at a young age. They had no protection or no one to turn to, so this is what they had to accept. This scarred them and affects the way they interact with men even as a grown woman. Many were lost along the way and got caught up in sex at a young age, and even those that didn't do it willingly still suffered because maybe they were raped. If you are this girl then this is probably sitting right in your lap and if it is ask yourself these questions. Was I molested at a young age? Was I brainwashed by older boys at a young age? Did I give in to sex because I thought it was expected of me? Did I get pregnant before my 18th birthday? Did I get raped before my 18th birthday? Have I stripped or had sex for money? If you answered yes to all of these questions or to all but one or two, my heart goes out to you. This is why your beauty won't stop your man from cheating on you. It's not your fault but yet it still hurts that man to know you've been with men unwillingly or illegitimately and because of that he has no sense of ownership so he searches for it with women on the side.

I've touched on the major reasons why beauty can't stop a man from cheating and the reasons why it's almost impossible for a woman to have it all. We as people are shaped by our experiences. That's why Queens aren't humble as servants and servants aren't arrogant as Queens. Your beauty is what it is and that's what it has made you and because no beauty can be perfect, your beauty can't keep a man faithful.

CHAPTER SIX

Why Is It So Easy For Guys to Leave a Relationship?

Contrary to popular belief a man takes a break up harder than a woman, even if the man is the one who initiates the break up. The fact that a man doesn't openly show his emotions makes dealing with things a lot harder than it does for women. A woman can break down and cry anywhere and it is accepted. That means whenever she is hurting she can just cry it out, no matter where she is or what she is doing and that is ok. On the other hand, a man has to do it in his closet or when he is all alone. That makes it harder for a man to get over his problems. Where a woman can cry all day everywhere she goes, a man has to save his tears until he gets home. Just because it seems like that man is not disturbed, on the inside he is torn apart and about to boil over with emotions. What I will touch on mostly in this answer is the up grade rule and my theory that the only way to forget something old is to replace it with something new.

When a man has a woman he is only focused on her until he gets to know her. For every man it takes a different amount of time, meaning that for one man it may be six months and for the next man a year and the next man five years. No matter the amount of time, that is all the time you get from that man. After a man is use to you and you are very predictable to him and the sex is boring and nothing exciting is happening then he starts looking for your replacement. To find a replacement could take years, so you can be with a man five or ten years thinking that he is in it for the long run but really the reason is because he hasn't been able to find someone else that intrigues him more than you did. Instead of just being alone he stays with you so he can still have a partner, regular sex, and things along those lines. No one wants to be alone and miserable. It's sad because he is plotting his escape and you have no idea.

Understand that while you are with your man, he is looking around trying to find the next woman he can get to know. He will venture into the lives of many different women looking to see if she has something you don't. This won't be something sexual, it gets deeper than that. For example, you may be in college and studying to be a lawyer or a doctor. You also have your own car, and you live in college apartments. On top of all that you are a descent looking person. Then one day he meets a girl that is studying to be a doctor also, but her car is a little nicer than yours, her rent is a little higher than yours, and she is just as pretty. That makes that woman an upgrade from you. This is what can take his interest away from you and allow him to move on. While he's getting to know her he could be getting ready to make his transition from you to her. All of a sudden, he realizes she isn't as clean and neat as you, so he lets her go and puts his focus back on you. Now he's appreciating your cleanliness a little more than he did before because he's had something to compare it to. Later he could meet a woman that is studying to be a lawyer, she has a car, her own place, and she's prettier than you. Then once again he is getting ready to make his transition from you to her. All of a sudden, he realizes that she is bull headed and stubborn while you are humble and submissive. He then lets her go and comes back to you appreciating your humility more than ever. Understand that he keeps pulling away and then coming back strong and seeming so in love. This keeps you on an emotional roller coaster but at the same time is intriguing to you and keeps you on your toes. You're playing right into his trap and you love him like never before because he keeps coming out of the blue, loving you like crazy, and putting you on cloud nine. All the while your relationship isn't fazing him at all. He just has to adjust and give you another brownie point for being more unique than the next woman. All he has to do is just keep looking. He could go through a hundred women before he finds one that is better than you all the way around. Then and only then is when he'll leave. He won't leave you for someone that isn't as good as you, which would be stupid of him. This is why I call it an upgrade. To a man you're just like a car or his clothes. After a while they get old and you have to upgrade to something bigger and better to feel fresh again.

My mother told me to never speak numbers in regards to my love life, but if I didn't I wouldn't be being completely honest and then I would be just like every other man you've met and the point of this book is to be just the opposite. Once I was with a woman and it took me about two months to get use to her. Then we had to go home for the summer and with her not being there I couldn't hold out on my life. I wasn't sure we'd work out so I kept looking. In the mean time she got my name tattooed on her and I was in the process of looking for a new girlfriend. Then we went back to school and she said she had to make a confession. She made me promise that I wouldn't get mad and that I would get over it as soon as she told me. I promised to that. She then admitted to going to a movie with a friend of her sister and also going to a party where her ex-boyfriend was in attendance also. I thought to myself "are you serious". She had to take deep breaths and everything before she told me. Then I said ok well I have some confessions too. I gave her the same stipulations that she had given me. Then I told her that I had been with nine different women in that three month hiatus. She just swallowed deep and we brushed it off. Of course later it hit her very hard and she released the emotions she had held back at the moment I told her. She stayed with me though and that made me love her even more because of that. That wasn't good enough to have a woman that would stay with me after nine other girls. I messed with another in that semester and then went home for Christmas break and messed with 2 or 3 more. Then went back to school and messed with another. That next summer she came home and stayed with me to keep a close eye on me. Although she lived with me, I still managed to sleep with another girl twice right under her nose. Then we went to different schools the next fall and I went with six more girls. After all that, I still hadn't found an upgrade. Understand I hadn't confessed since I confessed to the first nine, so she was deep in love and living happy somewhat. She still had nightmares from the nine other women and had no clue it was more than that. To make a long story short, I went through 26 other women before I found my upgrade. I'll have you know this is about average if not a little below average for my peers. I was with her for two years and in those two years it took me 26 experiments before I found the right upgrade. When I found my upgrade, I just called her and told her it was over and moved on with my life. I ended up going back to her for a few months while my upgrade and I had our problems. I went back to her and she fell in love all over again and then me and my upgrade met back up and hit it off again. Then I called my fiancé and told her it was over for the second time and that time was for real.

I don't want you as a woman to think that I'm one in a million. I am just like every other man I've ever met when it comes down to women. I've done a lot and what I haven't done I've seen the rest. It's safe to say your man is just like me and right now while you're reading this if he's not beside you reading along he could be looking for his upgrade. Don't be naïve and believe you are better than any other woman around you and that he'll have to look a million years before he finds his upgrade. Please don't get complacent and think that just because you have his child, live in his house, or drive a car under his name that he won't up and leave without warning. After 25 years my father divorced my mother. I've been curious to know how many women it took him before he found his upgrade. Or if his upgrade was a woman or goals and ambitions, but one thing I do know as soon as he found her or it, it was over.

So you see, what makes it so easy for a man to leave a relationship is his upgrade. In order to forget something old you must replace it with something new. This is what every man knows. Otherwise you'd end up going back to that same old fling. A man bides his time watching and waiting for the woman that will sweep him off his feet and give him the strength he needs to move on. When I left my fiancé, I thought about her for nights on end but as long as my upgrade was on her game and keeping me interested I couldn't allow myself to move backwards. The reason a man leaves you so easy is because he has other options, while you are saying to yourself "he doesn't even care". Please believe that he cares probably more than you do, but the reason you can't see it is because his time is occupied somewhere else. I can assure you that every waking moment that his upgrade isn't by his side you're the only thing on his mind and he has to fight himself not to call you and make up. You can be sure that if he does leave with ease and then all of a sudden he's back knocking on your door, it's because his upgrade turned out to be a down grade but it took him a while to figure it out.

Please know that it has nothing to do with you as a woman when a man leaves you and doesn't look back. It's what he's found that is keeping him occupied and satisfied. With that said, condition your heart to run the long race and endure to the end. Every relationship has ups and downs and majority of the time it is due to the other woman in his life. If your man gets up and leaves you with no remorse while you sit and cry your eyes out day after day and then one day he comes back, remember what you read here today. Remember that just like he left you with ease one time he can do even easier a second time. It may take years and that's what some women let fool them. If you look around you'll find many women that had a man that took 20 or more years before he found his upgrade. Very rarely do you hear of the woman leaving the man. Your man could have a stroke or a heart attack and become a paraplegic and you still stay with him. If the shoe was on the other foot, you could end up very lonely. I'm not saying freeze your heart and shut your man out. I'm saying condition your heart for the worse and hope for the best.

Just like with every problem there are some possible solutions. From a man that has up and left with out even leaving a note, my advice would be to stay unpredictable. Just like you've read in other chapters or you will read, stay one step ahead of the game. Don't allow yourself to go into a lull and let your love life lose its flame. Study your man and know what he likes and think outside of the box. You have to set yourself up to a point that a woman would have to go to the moon and back to sweep your man off his feet. If other women are wearing boots, then you wear tennis shoes. If the fling you found out about has extensions then extend yours longer and put curls in it. If she shops at Body Shop then you go to Express, do what you have to do to keep the edge. For example, most men drink, smoke, or curse, knowing that I do none of the three. Most men hide their feelings so me knowing that I write poetry. Most men have too much pride to cater to their woman, knowing that I cook my wife breakfast and get her unexpected flowers and jewelry. This ensures me that in order for her to find a man better than me she will have to search the entire globe to do so. Therefore, in order to prevent your man from leaving you without out a warning or walking out and never looking back, set yourself apart. Go above and beyond the call of love and do things that you know other women won't do. The quote for my senior class in high school was "do today what others won't, so tomorrow you can do what others can't". That quote means so much and can take you so far in so many different aspects of life.

CHAPTER SEVEN

Why does a man beat on a woman?

There could be many reasons why a man beats on a woman and for many men the reasons are the same. The reasons I will touch on is what I believe to be the biggest reasons why a man beats a woman. As a woman you should never blame yourself or feel like you deserve to be beat. There is nothing you can do that should give a man the right to beat on you. I don't believe a man should be an enforcer to his other half. Its one thing to be the head but it shouldn't be by force.

One reason a man beats on a woman, is because that is what he saw his father do to his mother. As a young man you look up to your father and everything you see him do is instilled in you, and sometimes men become the same men their fathers were even though they may not want to. If a man watches his father become physical with his mother in order to gain respect or run his house then that boy will grow up and run his home that same way. We are all puppets on a string and we only do what we have seen someone else do. Therefore, for many men their father is the reason they beat on the woman in their life.

Another reason is because of the life that man has led. If a man was a submissive and passive child and teenager, then he took a lot of stuff that a man is not use to taking. There are many boys that you knew that would get jumped or beat up at school. Or maybe they were in the in crowd but they weren't seen as a tough guy. They could have been the pretty boy or the rich guy so that made them cool. Naturally that man was soft as a young boy and as a teen and did everything in his power to avoid confrontations with other men. Either he was terrified by the brutality of fights or physical sports or he felt weak and inferior to other guys his age. For this reason that young man concealed his feelings and his hate because he was the lesser of his peers. He had no one he could look down on or over power. Therefore, when he was enraged it had to be suppressed within because there was nothing he could do about it. This same young man may have bullied his female siblings if he had any or his younger family members so he could feel powerful in some way. Let me paint you a picture, if you take a can of sweet smelling air freshener and you put it in a hot shed outside and everyday it gets hotter and hotter, one day it is going to explode. The same happens with that young man. He is soft to begin with and on top of that he is forced to suppress his feelings of anger and rage every time something bad happens. Eventually one day when he is able to over power someone he will do just that. This is what forms an abusive man. As you may have learned in a class or two, people are products of their environments. Men who suffered that form of abuse will grow to be abusive. I can speak from experience, because I was once that little boy. I was raised with a mother and a father so I didn't have to struggle. Without that struggle, I wasn't forced to become tough and fend for my own. I was very well taken care of. I was from a quiet home and raised to be meek and humble, therefore I didn't speak up for myself nor did I want to fight for what was mine. Many times I walked away from fights and bottled my anger. When I did fight I never lost a fight, but that was because I released on that person what I had held in for so long. I rarely fought because I didn't like the brutality of it. Therefore, my experience has helped me hone in on this subject. I grew up to be an abusive man with one of my counterparts. I had held in so many frustrations for so many years when I finally was the bigger of the two and the more powerful of the two, I took advantage of it. As sad as it is to say and as much of a shock it may be for those who know me, I am man enough to admit it. In order for a man to come out of it he must first be able to admit it. I know a lot of men just like me, but they are afraid to admit that they too let their own self hate get the best of them. The testimony is I came out of it. A man doesn't grow out of it, he has to face himself in the mirror and confront himself so that he can become a real man. I decided to let that relationship go and turn over a new leaf and become brand new again. This time I am living my life as a real man, a man that is too much of a man to hit someone weaker than me.

As I said, I had to come out of that relationship because inside of it I could have never changed. It was something in her spirit that didn't connect with mine. No matter how delicate it was it would trigger a rage inside of me to explode and make me into a beast. That is why I feel the need to warn every woman that reads this and is in an abusive relationship. The only way for it to stop is for you to come out of it. Once a man has a connection to abusing you then that's the only way he can express himself when he is angry unless he just stops caring at all. If you are in an abusive relationship you can probably recall when it started as just a push. Next, it was a choke. Then it was a push and a choke. Later it turned into slaps and punches or body slams of some sort. Just like any negative behavior that isn't stopped it will only get worse. I tell every woman I know that is in an abusive relationship to get out, because no matter how long it takes one day it'll result in death. A man will continue to escalate and go one step further every time. I watched it happened in me and then I've watched it happen in the relationships of my loved ones. I have aunts with permanent swollen lips and eyes because of abusive relationships. I have aunts with deformed body parts because of broken bones that were never fixed. They came out of that relationship and that is the only reason why they are alive today. Domestic violence is very serious and should never be taken lightly. I thank God for delivering me from the vice grip the devil had on my life. Now, my wife can vouch for me and say that I am a real man that handles my problems like a man. I am no longer afraid to confront myself or my problems like a man. It isn't a matter of a man being afraid of other men. Now, it's a matter of that man being afraid of him. He knows that there is something defective in him that if he goes off he could annihilate whatever is in his path without even blinking. That is why he must be able to confront himself.

As a woman, you have to know your man. Communication is the key. Engage in conversations that will answer the questions you need to know about his personality. If he is a no non-sense person then take him at his word value and respect that. As a woman, you have to understand that a man lives by his pride and his pride alone. If you are with a man that is not naturally abusive and shows no signs of why he should be, there is still a possibility that you can be abused. There are some ways you can avoid it though. Start by being able to effectively communicate. Respond to a man's voice that way he will not have to go any further. If a man is speaking and trying to express himself be quiet and listen to what he has to say no matter how harsh it may be. This way he won't have to use his hands because you are listening to his voice. It is hard for a man to hit anything that looks helpless. If you are listening to him and you are making direct eye contact, like you learn in communication class, he won't have a reason to want to hit you. What makes a lot of men hit their women is the fact that they won't listen. If he yells and you yell right back you challenge him as a man. If he is talking and you talk over him, you challenge him as a man. If he moves to escape and you step in front of him, you challenge him as a man. If he curses at you and you curse back at him, you challenge him as a man. With a man you must follow certain rules of engagement. It's important that you remember how a man thinks and operates and if you can't respect him as a man then you shouldn't be with him. If you provoke a man to hit you just like another man does, then he'll hit you like he'd hit another man. Give your man the decency of having his manhood. That way if he is not naturally abusive you won't have to worry about him becoming that way.

Now if you read this and you can honestly say you do all those things correctly and that you give your man no reason to go any further than a conversation, but he still beats you then its time for you to leave. If a man can't solve a problem with you by talking it out then you shouldn't be with him. If a man jumps to conclusions without hearing you out and taking you at your words value like you do for him, then you shouldn't be with him. Any man that has to resolve a problem with a woman through physical abuse is not a real man, and deep down he knows it. The best thing you can do for him is leave. Many women condone abusive behavior by accepting it and reinforcing it. When I was in an abusive relationship, my counterpart would reward my abuse with sex. Therefore I would have never come out of that stage of my life if I had left it up to her. If she had ignored me after that or started distancing herself from me, then it would have brought me back to my senses a little bit. If your other half is abusive show him you don't appreciate it by distancing yourself from him. Cut off your love and communication with him. It'll either cause him to become more violent or change because he knows he is losing you, The sad thing is if you go back, then eventually he'll go back to the same abusive man he was before. Then you are forced to leave him. Remember any man who truly loves you will never lay a hand on you!

CHAPTER EIGHT

What Are Some Reasons
Black Men go White?

This is a very deep question and a lot of women have asked this question. There isn't any one answer to this question and each man will have his own personal reason, even if he can't identify with it. I can speak for myself on this question because there was a period in my life that I ventured this way. I believe that my reasons are the same reasons as the many black men I've met that date white women. Although many men don't question themselves nor do they bother to answer those who question them either, I truly feel that if any man who dates white was to read my reasons they would identify with them.

I'll start off by separating black women and white women as their own separate entities. You as a black woman or a white woman are very different from your sisters of the opposite color. Just like many questions the answers lye in history, and in this case so does the difference in black and white women. Let's look back into the days of slavery in America. You have the black woman who was a servant to her white master and the white woman who was a servant to her white master. The catch is they served in two very different ways and this shaped these two women completely different. A black woman was forced to pick cotton in the heat of the day right next to her man with her kids trailing behind. This black woman had to be just as strong as her male counterpart. She was expected to perform the same duties that he had to with no exceptions. Because of this, black women were built tough and forced to stand on their own two feet. At any moment their other half could be sold to another master or killed by his master. This woman had to weather the storm and be able to stand regardless. A black woman was made a strong individual by the things she suffered and she would pass that same strength and integrity on to her daughters and granddaughters. This is how we get strong independent black women in the 21st century. I do believe that over the years black women have taken this strength and integrity and lost its essence. Now it is a proud spirit that ends in a fall. A black woman prides herself on having her own job, her own car, and her own place to live. A black woman is proud to say "I don't mind having a man, but I don't need a man". What she doesn't realize is that she is a product of her ancestors. Who toiled in the hot beating sun and worked their fingers to the bone right beside their man, while still respecting him as a man. Now we have very independent and stubborn black women.

On the other hand, you have the white woman who was also a servant but she was married to the master. The white woman was there to aid her master in whatever way she needed to, while knowing he was sleeping with the black slave women. She stood by him and took care of her children. The white women were there to cook breakfast, lunch, and dinner or order the black maid to do so. As a white woman she was free of labor, stress, and the strength that comes with it. A white woman was the helper to her man. Her duties were to clean the house and make sure the kids were well fed and cleaned daily. This white mother would teach her daughter how to cook and clean for her man and show her by example how to listen and respect a man. The white mother brought her daughter up to cater to her man in order to get a wealthy and established white man. She also was taught that black men were as forbidden fruit and was never to be touched. Think of this as an analogy liking unto Eve and the forbidden fruit. We as humans want what we can't have. Because of the lineage of white women today, we have obedient, submissive although deviant white women. White women aren't bound by color barriers any more and they can eat the fruit of any tree they please.

That is the difference between black and white women. I found by looking back to what each woman was made from, I was able to understand who they are today. The reasons why a black man goes white is almost obvious in some ways. The least of the reasons would be revenge. As a black man sometimes we feel like we are held down by the white man, in order to beat them in America we have to be twice as good. Not every black man wants to rap or play sports but that's the areas white men said we can have. Some black men want to be doctors and lawyers or an author of a best seller. In America those jobs could be seen as a white man's job because it takes a good education and because of slavery many black men are behind the learning curve. Some black men may want what a white man has in some areas of his life. If he can't get that then he'll settle for his women. Every black man knows there is nothing a white man hates more than to see a black man with a white woman. If that's a man's reason then it has nothing to do with a black woman. In essence that black man has nothing against his own kind; he's just caught up fighting his battle with the wrong weapon.

Another reason black men go white, is to see what its like. I've learned through my studies that, men are not racist towards women. Almost any color man will sleep with any color woman. To a man sex is sex and there isn't much difference between the races. Some black men just wonder if the grass is greener on the other side of the fence. Therefore, he jumps the fence with no intentions of staying but sometimes gets trapped on that side. I believe the men who do it as an experiment plan to return to his own and marry his own; he just wants to see what it feels like. A man is from a line of men who were able to have hundreds of wives and concubines of all different races and colors. Just like any experiment you test it more than once until you are able to prove your hypothesis. Later you come to a conclusion and you move on.

Lastly, I feel the main reason a black man goes white is because of the differences between the two races. Some black men have controlling personalities and many black women aren't going to put up with that unless she was raised like a white woman. I've dated that type of black woman also. That was very interesting but that's a whole different story. Many black men want to feel like a King after a long days work, but just like the days of slavery the woman may have worked just as hard. My mother was famous for this line, "I work just like you do!" My father would be frustrated and tired because he worked in the hot sun all day and my mother worked in the air conditioner, but she wouldn't cook or clean when she came home.

Then you look in the white household and many white mothers don't have to work. They are what we call housewives. They live just like they did in the days of slavery and their only job is to cater to her man. When a black man ventures that way he is leaving a woman that when he says "can you clean the room", she says "your hands and legs ain't broke you clean it". He goes to a woman that when he says "can you clean the room", she says "yeah I'll clean it no problem". To hear that response feels so much better and it makes you feel so much more like a man. You automatically go back to when we were Kings.

While inside of this lifestyle there are numerous scenarios in which these two women will react completely different and majority of them are in favor of the white woman. A white woman will go where you tell her to go and do what you tell her to do with no questions asked. For your birthday and Christmas, she showers you with gifts and makes you feel like a King. With many black women I've met they would rather receive than to give and when they do give they won't go broke doing so, but white women will. When a black woman receives she almost expects her man to go beyond her expectations. White women are intimidated by black men because they know the stock we are made from. They come to a black man to find a sense of security that she couldn't find with a white man; therefore she serves that man happily. Black women are not intimidated by black men at all. This is because she comes from a line of women that had to do the same work a man did. I'm sure you've seen a black female swear up and down she will fight a man and bluff as if she can physically keep up with him in a fight. It's funny when you think about it. She doesn't realize it's not true until she catches a blow that brings her back to reality. White women won't even test it because she already is in fear of that man. These differences are why black men go white and end up staying on that side of the fence. It may be sad to a black woman but it's true.

When you see a NBA player or a doctor and lawyer go to a white woman, just know it's because he feels black women are too much of a headache for his career. He would rather come home and be the boss after a long hard day than have to come home to fight for territory and declare his manhood in his own home. So the reason is not because he wants to give more to someone that already has the world, as I've heard many black women say. It's simply because of the difference in the way the women react to their man. Some black men are not strong enough or built to share his throne or split the jeans so that both can wear a pair. He'd rather be the head and have a tail than have two heads of the same body.

As black a woman in order to prevent this from happening to you there are some changes you would have to make. I'll have you know I came back to my own; I have a beautiful black Queen who realizes there is no room for pride in love. She made the changes many black women need to wake up and make, so they don't end up single or see their man leave them for a white woman. As a black woman, you have to realize that it is ok to have a man take care of you. It's ok to listen and let a man lead if you know he loves you. If he loves you then put your heart in his hands and trust him not to break it. God built a man to lead and that is why we were Kings and why we are Presidents. If you are a woman and you have a man, you expect him to "man up" in hard times. When all is going wrong and you don't know what you are going to do next, you turn to him and lean on him for his strength. If you can do that in a time of need then you need to be able to do that when all is well also. It's not fair to a man if you don't want to listen and cater to him when everything is fine then as soon as you need your rent or your car note paid you run to him for his help.

If you are single, ask yourself if you listened to your man. Ask yourself if you did what he asked you to do when he asked you to do it. Ask yourself if you argue back and forth with him on a regular basis. If the answers are yes, then that could be why you are single today. I asked my wife to let me lead and to trust me not to lead her in the wrong way. I told her that I would love her whether we were up or down and no matter what I would be the man of our household. I have bought her many gifts and paid many of her bills and it upset me that when we would disagree I couldn't be heard as a man. I told her if anything I've earned the right to be heard, I've bent over backwards and sacrificed enough that I deserve to be respected as a man. One day she realized that I really do love her and she gave me her load to carry and I bare that on my back everyday with pride knowing that no matter what I say my wife will listen. There is no greater feeling than for a man to feel like he is the man. If you refuse to listen to your man, refuse to do the things he asks of you and you insist on arguing and having the final say in the decisions of your lives together, you strip that man of his pride and his sense of manhood. That is the only thing God gave a man that he can't live without. If you know that man loves you with all of his heart and you feel that he wouldn't do anything to hurt you, then love and let go of your pride. We are not slaves any more and you don't have to work as hard as your man. The world is changing and allowing black men to be just as wealthy as white men. If you want to be that man's woman instead of seeing another good brother go white then it's up to you. You have to be humble and submissive enough to let a man feel like the man in order to keep that man.

I will end this chapter with a quote from the Bible. This comes from I Corinthians 13:4-8 and it reads "Love suffers long and is kind; love does not envy: **love does not parade itself, is not puffed up; Does not behave rudely, does not seek its own, is not provoked, thinks no evil**; Does not rejoice in iniquity, but rejoices in the truth; **Bear s all things, hopes all things, endures all things**. Love never fails".

CHAPTER NINE

Why is it that men cheat with less attractive women?

This is a funny but good question. The answer is simple though. When your man cheats with a woman that isn't as pretty as you it's because he's not looking to replace you, he's just trying to spread his wild oats. Or get a point across. For a woman that looks as good as you or better then it would take the same amount of time it takes with you, but for a woman that is beneath you then its usually quick and easy. I'll touch on the difference in flings and the reason a man has flings. Everything about this answer is important and vital to you understanding a man's thought process behind cheating.

First you have the cute fling. This girl is a girl that your man can see himself being with and he takes his time with her. This is the girl that he will call his friend or his homie. This is the girl that he will spend quality time with whether it is in person or on the phone. This is the girl you will have to accept because if not he'll just leave you and focus on her and he almost makes it clear to you. This is the friend that you know about but you probably haven't seen her nor does he want you to see her. He just emphasizes that they are just friends and that's that. She knows all about you and is cool with your man just being her friend although she may like him. In a way she counts on him to make all the moves if any, therefore she doesn't have to get beat up for trying your man. This woman most likely has a life of her own because a cute fling won't wait around on a man and is usually in a relationship and just trying new things for a while. This is the female that you don't have to worry about anything physical happening with, because when its time for that you can assure he won't be with you. When he knows it's time for that you and him will most likely take a "break" or just break up. He may plan to come back to you after he gets what he wants from the cute fling, she doesn't know that but she won't do anything with him until he is rid of you. That way she doesn't have to worry about feeling like she is second string. Cute flings are demanding so it's either just friends or they want it all, nothing in between. Therefore no "friends with benefits" there will only be emotional cheating with this woman. This is the worse type of fling because this fling can actually ruin your relationship without you even knowing it's about to happen. This usually happens all of a sudden with no signs before it does, besides arguments that you may brush off as just normal relationship drama. When he's gone it doesn't mean he's not coming back but it is usually because of that cute fling.

Then on the other hand you have the ugly fling. When I say ugly, I don't mean unbearable I mean not as cute as you. This is what this question is all about. You may have been cheated on and then you seen the girl on Facebook or My Space and your mouth dropped because you were wondering what in the world? This is what I call the ugly fling. This is the girl that either knows your man has a girl and doesn't care because she is desperate and believes she can take your place or is looking for a man very desperately. When a man cheats down it's usually because he is just bored and wondering if he still has it. He is wondering what it's like to be with another woman again. Sometimes that woman is just ugly to another woman, but the man could see something completely different when he's looking at her. I mentioned in another chapter a man may cheat because of one thing. That one thing could be virtually anything. It could be her car, her eyes, her apartment, her legs, her breasts, or any one particular thing. In a whole that woman may not be as cute as you but in that one area she is way cuter than you. She may have not so perfect teeth or she may have short hair and therefore you deem her as not cute. But she may have a butt like J-Lo and that's all your man was seeing. The rest really didn't matter because he just wanted to see what she looked like in a thong or butt naked so that's why he went with her. Remember a man won't leave you for another woman unless she is an upgrade; she has to be better than you in a whole, not just in one area. On the other hand, when it comes to cheating all she has to have is one thing that you don't have.

If the girl is truly not cute and there is nothing about her that is cute and you as a girlfriend or wife are not being bias, then most likely he just was doing it just to do it. As sad as it may sound sometimes we do it just to do it. When it's over we even question ourselves as to why we did it and was it worth it and the answer is often times no, but none the less we've already done it. Now that the deed is done there is no going back. Now we may think twice before we do it again, but there will come a time that we venture down that ugly road again. As women you can rest assure that your man will always come back from that and unless you leave him he won't stop. Most of the time when a man cheats down its because there is something he wants to test or something he wants to find out, so that girl is like a lab rat in sense. If a man who is handsome messes with a girl who is not cute, you can almost bet your bottom dollar it took little or no effort for him to do so. Therefore, his test or night of fun took nothing out of him and is easy for him to do it over and over again. At the same time, this could be to send you a message.

He could know that you will find out and just ask why and still be with him, so he does it to make you step your game up. He does it to let you know he can do it and to show you that you don't have his heart yet. Therefore, you have no room for complacency. If you are still with your man and you are asking yourself this question, then that is where you've gone wrong. That is the reinforcement he needs to do this same thing to you over and over. After a while, this will become very belittling and this will demoralize you in a way that may take you a very long time to regain your self esteem.

A downgrade is easy in any way you look at it. It takes nothing of a man and means nothing to him. An upgrade is what takes time and that is what takes effort. Knowing that a man will cheat, it is better to know he is cheating down rather than trying to cheat up. When he begins to try to cheat up that is when you have to worry.

I would like to ask you. Have you ever been cheated on? When your man cheated did he cheat up or down? After he cheated did you remain in that relationship? If he cheated down how did it make you feel? After he cheated up how did it make you feel? Do you know if he cheated up or down?

All of those questions are important questions to ask yourself, because how you respond to your man's cheating will determine if and when or how he will cheat again. If he cheats down and you stay with him, what message does that send him? If he cheats and you step up your game, what message does that send him? Either way, if you stay you are sending a message that will end up your worst enemy. I've cheated on women before and then made it known to them in a confession session of some sort. A woman never left me for cheating and I know a lot of women who stay in a relationship after she has been cheated on. This only reinforces that man's behavior and it empowers him to do the same thing over and over. Therefore you have to rock the boat in a sense in order to see a change. I do not believe there is much a woman can do to stop a man from cheating but I do believe there are some things a woman can do that can divert his cheating scheme. If your man has cheated down and you were blown away wondering why, then flip the script and see if ugly is what he wants. Of course you know its not but it will send him in another direction. If your man has cheated then instead of stepping up, step down. After he has cheated and you are made aware of this, go from Miss Beautiful to Miss Hideous. Wear sweat pants and big tee shirts. Don't do your hair or your make up and force him to look at you. When he wants to take you out to make up, go out looking like you just got out of bed and since he is the one who made the mistake he will have to accept you just as you are. This will send him in the wrong direction. To him you will seem like you are torn apart and maybe you are, but instead of hiding it let it show. Show the other side, the not so beautiful side. Then when he asks why you are dressing that way and why you don't fix yourself up, tell him you thought he liked uglier girls. A lot of women do the opposite and don't realize that this is reinforcing to that man. This tells him that when you slack up all he has to do is cheat and you'll get back on your game. He will then use this as a tool to blackmail you and play you like a pawn. If your man see's that cheating pulls you away from him and makes you get down on yourself, this will cause him to slow down a bit. Next time, he will think before he tries to cheat.

Whether it's up or down if you stay with a man after he has cheated then most likely he'll continue to do it. I know you may be in to deep to leave and you may just say you don't care and live like that. When you do that you will push him away and then you are asking to be replaced. When you begin to find that complacency then he'll start to cheat up looking for your replacement. When a man cheats and it is with a girl that is not cute, appreciate the fact that he isn't looking to leave you. He is just looking for a fling. If you wish to stop it then you have to become more involved in his life and keep him on edge when it comes to your sex life with him. Try new things and be his freak. When you want to keep your man to yourself you have to be his everything. You have to be his stripper, his porn star, his video girl, and his runway model. Push the bar and force yourself to grow and step outside of your comfort zone. That way you won't have to worry as much about him fulfilling lust with ugly girls, because he can fulfill them with you. When it all boils down to it, it's up to you. You can keep your man home more and you can keep him out of the ugly girl's pot of goodies if you allow him to get all he wants out of yours.

To reiterate the reason, a man cheats with an ugly girl because he is looking to fulfill a lust or to send a message and really just to see if he can do it. An ugly girl can not be a threat to your relationship. You'll never see a man leave a swan for an ugly duckling. But he will use the ugly duckling to make the swan jealous and make the swan question herself as to say "am I not that pretty"? Or, "is she as pretty as me"? A lot of men have goals to demoralize you, to make you think he is all you can have and that outside of him you have no hope. This will ensure him that you won't leave him, because he has your mind. As long as you think that you are not even pretty enough to keep him home then he knows you won't ever think you're pretty enough to leave. I know when that happens that makes you question yourself about who you are and what you look like and that is the worst thing you can do. Never question yourself when your man decides to step outside of the relationship. That is in a man and he does that inevitably no matter who you are, what you look like or how you dress a man will be a man. Every man has cheated down at one time or another and out of the 10 men I asked why, they all said they just did it for the heck of it. Once again, that proved my theory to be right in my mind as to say that to many men just like me it never meant anything. It never meant that my girl wasn't pretty or that the fling was as pretty as my girl. The only time a man will cheat up is when he is ready to leave. As long as you can find out he is cheating and you know that she isn't as pretty as you, just know it's meant to demoralize you and force you to step up or step out. What will you do next time it happens?

CHAPTER TEN

Will A Man Ever Stop Cheating?

Yes, for a period of time although I don't think it will last very long. I believe that a man is most faithful when he begins a new relationship. The reason is because he's occupied with the task of getting to know that woman and letting her get to know him. The man is focused on one task and he can't focus on more than one and give both his all. Therefore, in order to start a relationship off right and let that woman know that he is all about her, he must spend every free second of his day with her in some way. It may not be in person but it will be over the phone. If he's not with you or talking to you then he'll be out doing something for you like washing your car or buying you a small gift. This is the claiming and naming process as I like to call it. After a man feels like he knows you then he is able to begin cheating because he has done what he had to do.

Here is an analogy for you to digest. You as a woman are like a new book to that man. Not just any book though. You are a book of a trade that he is very interested in learning. When he begins to read this book it will get all of his attention. Every free moment he has he will pick up that book and read some more. He is taking very detailed notes and committing everything to memory. He may even read the same chapter more than once to really comprehend all that it is telling him. While he's reading about this trade he can't read another at the same time and learn them both as well as he needs to. If he tries then most likely he'll get confused between the two and mix up the information. An over ambitious man may try but he'll fail at learning those two trades at the same time. A smart man will take his time on that first trade. If it takes him a year to learn it he'll focus and make sure he learns every intricate detail before moving on to another one. At the end of the book, if he feels he has mastered that trade he will practice on it and see if he can do exactly what he learned. If not he'll go back and read the chapters he didn't quite understand. After he has digested all the material and he is sure he knows what he's doing, he'll put that book down and begin on another. Granted, he still has that trade in his back pocket. He doesn't forget it or throw the knowledge away; he simply just starts to learn another. He knows the first one very well so he doesn't have to spend much time brushing up or going back to it. He can now focus on the new trade he's found.

I painted that picture to show you how easily this rule of life could be understood. Yes your man may not have always been a cheater, but if he knows you by now then most likely he's cheating. Sit and think a minute. Does he know me? Do I get the same time and affection I got in the beginning? These questions will show you whether he's cheating or not. I say it like this, if you have a sense that he is then he is. There is no way around it. Trust your woman's intuition; I've hardly ever known it to be wrong when it was judging me.

I once knew a man who had been a pastor for over 20 years. He was anointed and he was no doubt a man of God. He had been with his wife for longer than he had been preaching. He stood behind the pulpit every Sunday morning and delivered the word of God. If anything thing can stop a man from cheating it's the power of God. I am a firm believer that the ONLY thing that can keep a man from cheating is the strength that only God can grant him through his earnest prayers. This man was caught in the very act of adultery in the church office on the desk with the church secretary. Whoa, that's a lot to swallow. What is shocking about it is, he was in his 50's. You may think, what in the world would make a man want to cheat when he's that old and besides that but when he is a leader and a man of God. A young lady told me that she knows her father isn't cheating because he is to grown for that. All I could do is laugh because I knew just how wrong she was. My late grandfather was 89 when he died. My grandmother would tell me and others stories about how he would come into her room with his walker late at night and ask if they could be intimate. He was 88 at the time and my grandmother was 81, if I'm not mistaken. She would tell exactly how he approached her and exactly what he said. She said she denied his request every time but I'm not sure I want to know the truth if that isn't it. I mention that to show an even more extreme example of a man's sex drive. My grandfather was an alcoholic so maybe that could be an excuse, but I wouldn't excuse it. I don't think he was one of a kind and that he is the only man of his age that tried the same thing he tried. My wife tells me stories about the old men in the VA hospital when she was doing C.N.A. work. These men were the same age as my grandfather and many of them were married with wives at home. They still hadn't stopped dreaming of sex and the pleasure they could remember. As a woman you may know this to be true through your own male figures in your life, and if you don't then now you do. Now think about that and ask yourself again do you really believe a man stop's cheating.

From a man to a woman, here are my suggestions to you. Keep your man on his toes. Remember you're like a trade, every so often tweak the art of your trade and make it a little harder for him to learn it. Don't lose sleep trying to accomplish this because then your relationship can be very tiring. I'll make it easy for you and give you the tips you need to be able to keep him on his toes.

In a relationship, you have mind games and you have sex games. I'll start with the tips for the mind games. First of all, stay on your toes that way he will stay on his. Trust him but don't be stupid. If he comes in late two or three nights in a row with a different story don't just accept it. Question him in an almost interrogating way, this won't push him away, it'll intrigue him. If he answers you politely over and over in an almost sarcastic way he could be telling the truth or just a master at his craft. You'll have to know the man in order to know which one it is. If he's known to be a player he's lien, but if he was never known as a player he's telling the truth. If he gets upset and yells the answers or answers questions with questions, he's lying. Remember the truth will set you free. There is no anger in the truth. The truth is what it is and he won't get offended or plead the fifth. Therefore, if a man is being truthful, he can simply answer your questions and respect your concerns. If he's always over on the minutes on his cell phone every month but yet he has plenty of minutes, this should raise your antenna. If he is in business for himself and a very ambitious young man, you can never prove he's cheating through this. If he's an average Joe working a 9 to 5 with nothing else going on, then he's most likely cheating. Cover your bases and check the numbers he calls at odd times of the night or the numbers that he spends long amounts of time on the phone with. This doesn't make you psycho. If he has nothing to hide, he'll say go ahead and if he does then he won't allow you to do it. You'll have to do it on your own time. Be careful! Know your man because you're treading on unsheltered territory. If he's abusive you may get beat if you're traveling this way, but if he doesn't abuse you then the truth you'll find. Many women trick themselves into believing "oh not my man". Some say, "I don't think he's cheating because the majority of his time is spent with me". Or you say "I know he love's me and I have his heart". I promise you, check your bases and you'll find yourself sweeping away a lot of dirt. In all my life, I still haven't met a faithful man and I've done plenty of research to draw a conclusion. I've met so many girls who believed so strongly and before long came back and said "you were right". I'm not an "I told you so" type of man. I'm here to help you figure out what to do next. When it comes to the mind games always think one step ahead and always trust your gut.

Inside of the sex games in every relationship there are things you can do to keep your man intrigued. By doing this he won't get bored and it can curve his appetite for the suspense and thrill of cheating. By no means is this easy, but if you want a faithful man it's worth a try. If you stick with it you'll find your man coming home on time every night and staying under his minutes every month. When it comes to sex there are two kinds of women so find out which one you are and take tips I give you. To make it simple, I break it into two categories the gimme's and the gotcha's. Its slang for the "give me's" and the "I got cha's". If you are a gimme, you never initiate sex. If you are the gotcha, you are willing to ask for it or make a move that sends a direct signal to the man's penis saying "I want you". For a man who has a gimme, then a gotcha is the biggest turn on and vice versa.

Pay attention. You have to stay unpredictable to keep your man on his toes and keep him intrigued. If you are use to just spreading your legs when he is ready or just kissing back when he kisses you then you have to switch it up. For example, when you know he's coming over or coming home lay in the bed with a tank top and no bottoms. Don't even warn him that you have a treat for him. Just do it! So when he comes in and gets in bed with you and he reaches to grab you and feels you have no bottoms on, it will send him to the moon. A shock will go to his lower member and excite him in a way like no other. This may be some of the best sex you've had in your life because he's so turned on. The next day all he'll be thinking about is what you did and it'll make him rush home the next day even though he knows you probably won't do it two days in a row. That one thing could get old, but it'll take a while if you do it every other day or so. He'll keep running home because until he catches on to the pattern he won't know when it's coming. After you've done it a while, you'll be comfortable with it and you can step up to being completely naked and sleeping through the night just like that, staying close to him all night. This takes a man back to when we were Kings. Another gotcha trick you can use is when your about to take a shower, politely ask him if he can join you. You may have taken showers together before but if he invites himself or ask you then this will be like brand new. Practice that for a while. From there you can be creative and push your limits. In order to keep him in your "box" you have to think outside of the box.

Now if you're a "gotcha" and you're use to sending messages to your man letting him know you want to have sex, now you have to switch it up and do the opposite without pushing him away. This will turn into mind games but it will be so intriguing to him that it will make him want to be around you all the time, so he can figure out what has gone wrong and search for the way he can fix it. This will tie up all of his time and you're getting exactly what you want. The first thing you can do is lay away from him when you're in the bed together. Slide all the way over to your side of the bed and curl up. If your bed isn't big enough for that because you sleep in dorm beds then sit in the chair on the computer for an hour or so when he gets in the bed. This will send his mind in circles and generate a lot of questions. Answer him ever so politely so that in your voice he senses all is well but in your actions you are saying something completely different. Try that for a while and stop right when you see he's about had enough and he stops asking questions. That will draw him back in because he thought you were a lost cause so he gave up and then boom all of a sudden problem solved. During that time, you shouldn't withhold sex because that would be too much for him to swallow. Wait until the next step for that. After you've successfully played that game move on to the next and this is where you'll withhold sex from him. When you're lying in bed and cuddling with him, he'll be waiting for that sign so don't give it to him. Kiss back instead of kissing first. Keep your clothes on also. After a while, he'll go ahead and make the first move. Don't toy with him forever and let him get all worked up, then your asking to get cheated on. Tell him right after he starts, "I don't want to have sex tonight". This will throw him off and he may keep going thinking "whatever you say but we'll see". If he keeps going, then it's his fault and he can't say you teased him and didn't tell him right off. Stay strong and don't have sex. This will be another area for him entirely and it will make him wonder so much that he'll start doing all he can to get you back to normal. Now you're playing a step ahead of the game and the ball is in your court. Be smart, and be safe!

Note from the Author

Thank you for reading my book. I hope that it helps you in your dating life. Please take the things you've read and implement them in your life. Keep your head up and know that the only good man is the one that you push him to be. If you let him be the man that every other man is then that is what he will be. Elevate your lifestyle.

I will be writing another book of specific scenario questions. If you have a scenario question that could not be answered in these broad answers please contact me with your question and it may be in my next book.

My Contact Info:
tagaskin@mail.usf.edu
213-814-0456

Please contact me with any questions or comments that you may have. Interviews, book signings or guest appearances can also be arranged through those same contacts.

BE BLESSED!

Special Thanks To:

First I would like to thank God for being with me and gracing this project. I would like to say thanks to my wife Sheri Chanroo Gaskins for supporting this work and not holding all that she read against me. I knew that if I was with a weak woman she could leave me over a book like this, but my wife stood by my side and not only understood but had a hand in making this book complete. Next, I would like to thank Joslyn Giles for sparking the conversation that would lead to me writing this book. I appreciate the encouragement Joslyn. I would also like to thank Andrea Woodfolk for coming up with the wonderful title of the book. Andrea you were a much needed inspiration. I couldn't have come up with a title like that without you. Thank you Gewanda Johnson, my beautiful and brilliant cousin. Thanks Gewan for your response to the chapter I sent you. I value your opinion very much. I would like to thank my little sister Latesha Gaskins for proof reading the book and giving me honest feedback. I love you Tesha. I thank my Momma also for bringing me in this world and supporting everything I want to do in my life. I also would like to thank my best friend and CEO/Founder of Krosstown Productions for designing the cover of my book. Tiger I can always count on you to support whatever project I have in mind. I appreciate it more than you know. I would like to thank Wesley Barnett for his support in my dreams also. Wesley you're a true friend. Last and most importantly I would like to thank my father Tony A. Gaskins Sr. for guiding my life and teaching me all that I know and training my mind to think outside of the box and teaching me how to articulate the feelings of my heart. Daddy I love you so much and I appreciate everything you have done for me. If there was a definition for tough love your picture would be beside it. You are truly the man that I admire the most. THANK YOU ALL!

12161785R00076

Printed in Great Britain
by Amazon.co.uk, Ltd.,
Marston Gate.